Fact or Opinion?

A **fact** is something that has happened or is real.

Example: We breathe air.

An **opinion** is something someone believes or thinks.

Example: I think the air smells funny.

Underline the sentence that is a fact. Circle the sentence that is an opinion.

1. An owl is a kind of bird.

   Owls are the wisest birds.

2. Reptiles do not make good pets.

   Some animals are reptiles.

3. People can buy bread at a store.

   Homemade bread is much tastier than bread from a store.

4. Fried chicken makes a delicious meal.

   Chicken is a type of meat.

5. A pen pal is a person who writes letters.

   I think it is fun to receive letters.

6. Books are more fun than television.

   Some books tell about real people.

7. I think spiders are ugly.

   A spider is an animal with eight legs.

That's a Fact!

A **fact** is something that can be proven.

Example: Many people keep dogs or cats as pets.

An **opinion** expresses someone's feelings about a person, thing, or an idea.

Example: Dogs are better pets than cats.

Read each sentence. Write whether it is a *fact* or an *opinion*.

1. A bear is an animal. ________	2. Wood comes from trees. ________	3. I think trucks are better than cars. ________	4. Robins are prettier than blue jays. ________
5. Some birds fly south for the winter. ________	6. A clock is used to tell time. ________	7. Hats look silly. ________	8. Country music is great. ________
9. Pizza is delicious. ________	10. I think dresses are pretty. ________	11. A whale is a mammal. ________	12. Hamsters have fur. ________

What Will Happen Next?

Often clues in a story will help you predict what will happen next. For example, if the characters are putting on raincoats and talking about dark, heavy-looking clouds, you can guess it might rain in the story.

Read the following paragraphs.
Fill in the circle that best predicts what will happen next.

1. "Let's clean up," said Mrs. Perez. "It's nearly time to go home." Andre hurried to the pet corner to take care of the hamster. Just as he was fastening the door to the hamster cage, the fire alarm rang. The teacher and children quickly left the building. The hamster looked at the half-closed door and then

○ closed the door. ○ escaped. ○ went to sleep.

2. Ashley passed a pet store on the way home from school. In the window, she saw a cute puppy. Ashley put her hand on the window near the puppy. It jumped at her hand and licked the window, wagging its tail. Ashley

○ went in to see the pup. ○ ran away in fright. ○ drove a car.

3. April took her dog, Tasha, for a walk on the beach. What a beautiful day! There were many people out walking their dogs. Suddenly a black cat stepped out from behind a rock. Tasha

○ entered a race. ○ got on a train. ○ chased the cat.

Word Detective

Sometimes when you read, you see an unfamiliar word. To find out what that word means, you can use all of the words near it as clues.

Use the word clues in the sentences below to help identify the meaning of each **purple** word.

1. The artist created a **sculpture** out of clay. The **sculpture** was shaped like a giraffe.

   A sculpture is

   ◯ a costume ◯ a poster ◯ a statue

2. The people enjoyed the **concert**. The music at the **concert** was played by a band.

   A concert is

   ◯ a large building ◯ a kind of food ◯ a musical performance

3. When riding on the train, some **passengers** talked quietly while others read books.

   A passenger is a

   ◯ talker ◯ rider ◯ reader

4. The **boulder** rolled down the hill and blocked the road.

   A boulder is

   ◯ a large rock ◯ a person ◯ a small rock

5. We had to **interview** a friend. I asked her 20 questions in the **interview**.

   An interview is

   ◯ a meeting with someone to get information
   ◯ information you would find in a dictionary
   ◯ a party

Making New Words

A **prefix** is a group of letters added to the beginning of a base word. A prefix changes the meaning of the word. Here are some common prefixes.

Prefix	**Meaning**
dis	the opposite of
un	the opposite of; not
re	again
de	away from; off

Read each word in the word box. Add *dis* or *un* to each word. Then complete each sentence below with the new word.

Word Box			
______ even	______ order	______ obey	______ plug

1. You won't find the pen with your desk in such ____________________.
2. Jake does not ____________________ his mother.
3. Don't trip. The sidewalk is ____________________.
4. Be sure to ____________________ the toaster before you clean it.

Circle the word that best completes each sentence.

5. Put out the campfire. It's time to ____________________ and leave.

   rebuild   decamp   repay

6. Our flight has landed. Let's ____________________ now.

   decamp   deplane   debug

7. The school collapsed in the earthquake. Let's ____________________ it.

   rebuild   repay   reelect

Change That Word!

A **suffix** is a group of letters added to the end of a base word. A suffix changes the meaning of the word. Here are some common suffixes.

Suffix	Meaning
ous	full of; having
ful	full of; causing
less	without; lacking
able	capable of

Read each word in the word box. Add *ous*, *ful*, *less*, or *able* to each word. Then complete each sentence below with the new word.

Word Box

marvel ______ breath ______ peace ______ bend ______

1. The new toy racecar tracks are ______________________.
2. Sheila had a ______________________ time at the birthday party.
3. The ______________________ music drifted through the halls.
4. The students were ______________________ after running around the track.

Add a suffix from the top of the page to each word below. Write the meaning of the new word.

5. courage **ous** ______ **full of courage** ______
6. danger ______ ______
7. time ______ ______
8. treat ______ ______
9. wonder ______ ______

Syllable Symphony

Write the number of vowel letters you see in each word.
Then write the number of vowel sounds you hear in each word.

There are as many syllables in a word as there are vowel sounds in the word.

	Vowel Letters	Vowel Sounds
1. conductor	3	3
2. flute	______	______
3. trumpet	______	______
4. trombone	______	______
5. orchestra	______	______
6. tuba	______	______

Write the number of syllables in each word.

7. drums 1
8. music ______
9. concert ______
10. violin ______
11. piano ______
12. harmony ______
13. cymbals ______
14. guitar ______

Parts Apart

When the first vowel in a word is followed by two consonants, the word is usually divided into syllables between the two consonants.

Example: mag net   rib bon

Write the word in syllables.

1. ladder **lad der**
2. compound ______
3. orbit ______
4. hammer ______
5. publish ______
6. enter ______
7. arrow ______
8. center ______
9. gallop ______
10. mustard ______

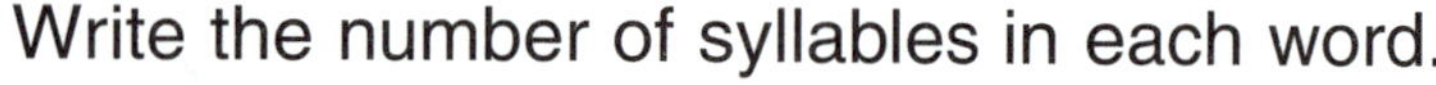

Write the number of syllables in each word.

11. hiking **2**
12. squirrel ______
13. sunflower ______
14. supervisor ______
15. together ______
16. whispering ______
17. suddenly ______
18. riverbank ______

What's the Idea?

In each paragraph below, circle the main idea and underline the supporting details.

1. Hiking in springtime can be interesting. Last May, I saw a mother bear and her three playful cubs across the river. I also saw a doe with her white-spotted fawn.

2. My dog greets me when I come home from school. We share snacks and sleep together in my bed. If I feel lonely, I can talk to my dog and she always listens. It's nice to have a pet.

3. Deserts are full of life. At first glance, it may seem as if nothing lives there. If you look closely, though, you will see animal tracks in the sand. Under rocks and in holes live small animals, insects, and reptiles.

4. Texas is an interesting place. It can take several days to drive across Texas. As you drive, you see many things. On the plains, cowboys round up cattle and drills bring up oil.

The Main Idea

Every paragraph has a main idea.
The other sentences give details that explain the main idea.

Read each main idea below and the sentences that follow it.
Fill in the circle next to each sentence that supports the main idea.

1. Penguins are unusual birds.

   ◯ Penguins stand upright on very short legs.
   ◯ Penguins walk with an amusing, clumsy waddle.
   ◯ Their scale-like feathers help keep them warm.

2. Emperor penguin fathers hatch and care for chicks.

   ◯ Killer whales like to eat penguins.
   ◯ Each dad holds an egg on his feet until it hatches.
   ◯ His feathers and skin help keep the egg warm.

3. Penguins have wings but do not fly.

   ◯ Their wings are small and have no flight feathers.
   ◯ These birds use their wings to swim.
   ◯ The water is really cold.

4. Some penguins have funny names.

   ◯ The female returns after two months of swimming.
   ◯ Macaroni penguins have strange head feathers.
   ◯ Little blue penguins come from Australia.

5. Penguins have different habits than other birds.

   ◯ Penguins spend much of their lives in the water.
   ◯ Penguins are excellent swimmers.
   ◯ On land, they build enormous nests called rookeries.

Soaring With Synonyms

Synonyms are words that have the same or almost the same meaning. Choose a synonym from the hot-air balloon to replace the **blue** word in each sentence.

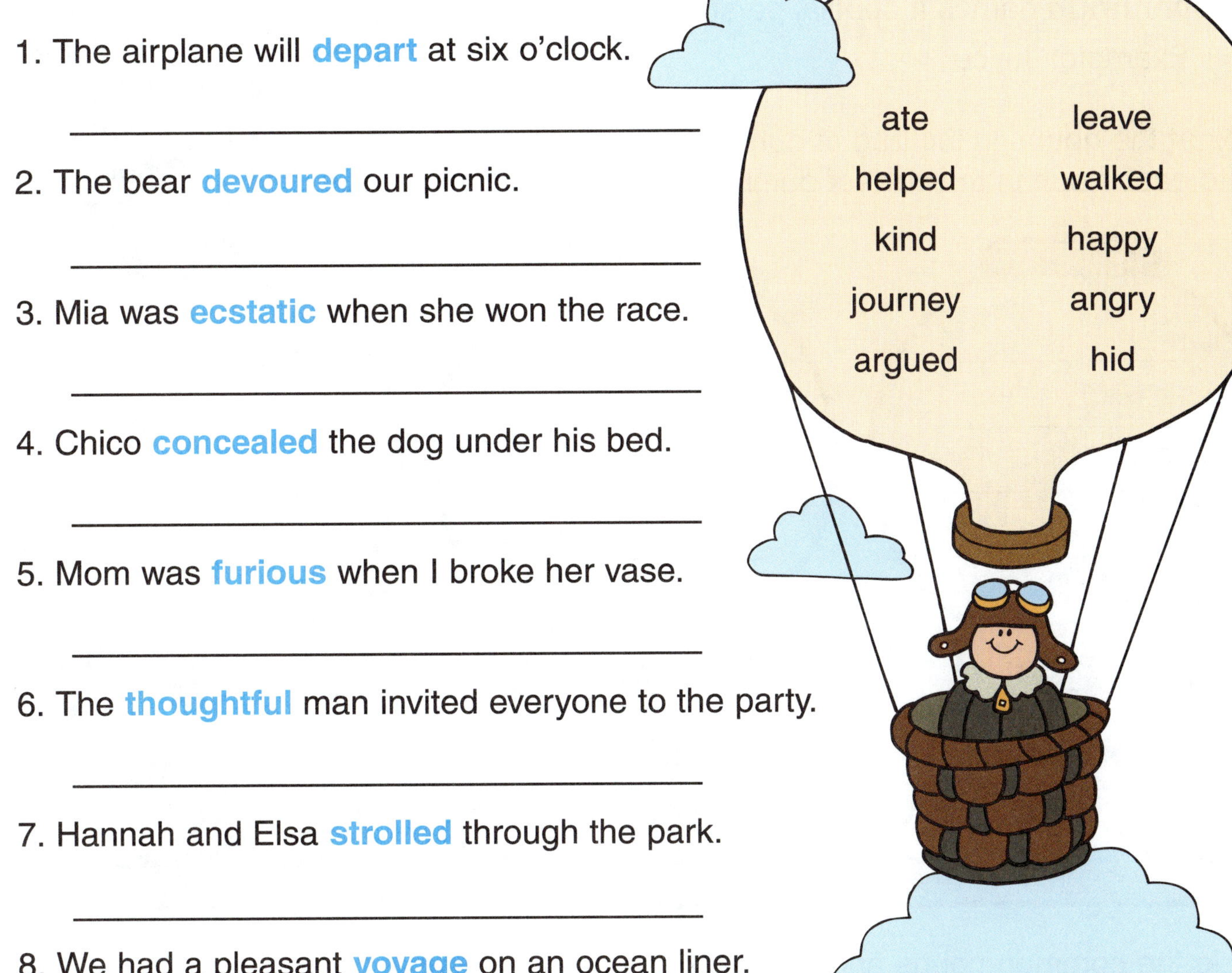

1. The airplane will **depart** at six o'clock.

   ____

2. The bear **devoured** our picnic.

   ____

3. Mia was **ecstatic** when she won the race.

   ____

4. Chico **concealed** the dog under his bed.

   ____

5. Mom was **furious** when I broke her vase.

   ____

6. The **thoughtful** man invited everyone to the party.

   ____

7. Hannah and Elsa **strolled** through the park.

   ____

8. We had a pleasant **voyage** on an ocean liner.

   ____

9. Roberto **assisted** Veronica in carrying the books to the library.

   ____

10. The boy **quarreled** with his mother about doing his homework.

   ____

Person, Place, or Thing?

A **common noun** names any person, place, or thing.

Example: girl

A **proper noun** names a special person, place, or thing.

Example: Joyce

Look at the nouns in the bag of gumballs.
Write each noun in the correct gumball machine.

hamster, Travis, China, brother, school, eraser, bike, Maria, firefighter, store, football, house

Circle the common nouns and underline the proper nouns.

1. Linda, come here.
2. Draw the picture, please.
3. Grandma is sleeping.
4. Patterson School is fun.
5. The clock ticked.
6. LaNell is happy.
7. Max laughed.
8. Did you find your book?
9. Balls bounce.
10. Buy that car.
11. Mice play.
12. Hit the net!

More Nouns

A **common noun** is the name of a person, place, or thing.

Example: mountains

A **proper noun** is the name of a special person, place, or thing.

Example: Canada

In each sentence below, underline the common nouns once and the proper nouns twice.

1. Italy is a beautiful country with famous buildings.
2. The queen has many little dogs.
3. The Olympics in Norway and France were beautiful.
4. My family is driving to the Grand Canyon for vacation.
5. On Saturday, we will have a picnic at Wildwood Park.
6. Emily ate pizza and ice cream at Little Flower School.
7. Doctor Smith listened to my heart.
8. Greece has some of the most beautiful islands.

In the space next to each sentence, tell whether the **orange** noun is a person, place, or thing.

9. The Gobi is a huge **desert** in Mongolia. ____________________
10. A koala is a small animal from **Australia**. ____________________
11. **Birgitt** was born in Germany. ____________________
12. Visitors to New York can see the **Statue of Liberty**. ____________________
13. **Guam** is an island in the Pacific Ocean. ____________________
14. The **sea horse** looks very different from most fish. ____________________

Spring Subjects

The **subject** is what or whom the sentence is about.
A subject can be one word or more than one word.

Examples: **Karla and Kim** went to Disneyland.
Disneyland was a lot of fun.
The roller coasters were the best part.

Underline the subject in each sentence.

1. We are glad spring came early this year.
2. The wildflowers are blooming along the country roads.
3. All the trees in my neighborhood have green leaves.
4. My favorite tree is a dogwood with white flowers.
5. I love to climb great big trees with lots of branches.
6. One of my friends has a secret tree house.
7. Our neighborhood club is called the Eagles.
8. We hold a meeting every Saturday in summer.
9. Mom and Dad are not allowed to come to our meetings.
10. They must be curious about what we do!
11. Mom and I planted a lot of tulip bulbs last fall.
12. The bulbs have now grown into flowers.
13. I especially like the red and yellow tulips.
14. My friends and I play baseball in the spring.
15. Jill is the best pitcher in our league.
16. I hope to hit a home run this season.

Name That Subject!

The **subject** of a sentence tells what or whom the sentence is about. A subject can be one word or more than one word.

Example: **Purple** is Laura's favorite color.
Laura's dress is blue and purple.

Read the sentences below. Provide a subject of your own for each sentence. Write it on the line.

1. ______________________ is my favorite color.
2. ______________________ is my best friend.
3. ______________________ tastes terrific.
4. ______________________ is my favorite sandwich.
5. ______________________ makes me so happy!
6. A ______________________ is the pet of my dreams.

Underline the subject of each of the following sentences.

7. Alex is so funny!
8. He always tells jokes.
9. Jake and I are his friends.
10. Alex's sister is talented, too.
11. She climbs trees.
12. Sue's talent is math.
13. Math is her favorite subject.
14. My favorite fish is swordfish.
15. Tom and Kim like to play soccer.
16. The two men laughed at the clown.
17. My neighbors enjoy working in the yard.
18. The library closes at six o'clock.
19. The milk was sour!
20. The computer broke down.
21. Penguins are fun to watch.
22. Steve and Jeremy rode their bikes.

What Is a Predicate?

The **predicate** tells what the subject does, is, or has. A predicate can be one word or more than one word.

Example: Morgan **likes squirrels**.

Circle the predicate in each sentence.

1. Michael packed a picnic lunch.
2. He rode his bike to his friend's house.
3. Kay and Michael walked to the park.
4. They played baseball.
5. They ate peanut butter sandwiches and cookies.
6. Then they climbed on the monkey bars.

Each sentence is missing a predicate. Write a predicate from the phrase box to complete each sentence.

Phrase Box

live in Calgary, Canada	build nests in springtime
sells ice cream	performs tricks with a rabbit
is gray today	got a new bike for my birthday

7. My friends ______________________
8. Birds ______________________
9. Max the magician ______________________
10. I ______________________
11. The sky ______________________
12. The ice-cream vendor ______________________

Complete That Thought!

An **action verb** shows what someone or something does.

Example: A cat **meows.**

Fill in the circle of the action verb that best completes each sentence.

1. When she ________ the car, it ran well.
   - ◯ drove ◯ spun ◯ skipped
2. I hope the plane ________ smoothly on our trip.
   - ◯ swings ◯ flies ◯ jumps
3. Rosie ________ when she gets hungry.
   - ◯ plays ◯ eats ◯ hides
4. In the warm sun, the oranges ________.
   - ◯ grew ◯ danced ◯ sang
5. The ocean waves ________ on the beach.
   - ◯ ran ◯ splashed ◯ fell
6. The tiny tiger cub ________ as it looked for its mother.
   - ◯ barked ◯ laughed ◯ cried
7. Some spiders ________ webs to catch prey.
   - ◯ spin ◯ destroy ◯ find
8. The horse ________ through the meadow.
   - ◯ galloped ◯ swam ◯ floats
9. The crowd ________ for its favorite team.
   - ◯ gathered ◯ competed ◯ cheers

In Place

A **pronoun** is a word that takes the place of one or more nouns.

Example: **Kristin** ate an apple.
She ate an apple.

Some pronouns are listed in the box below.

Word Box

he	she	they	we	his
him	her	them	us	it

Write the pronoun that replaces the **purple** noun. Use words in the Word Box.

_______________ 1. **Jeff** ate a hot dog at the baseball game.

_______________ 2. I enjoy eating **cotton candy** at the circus.

_______________ 3. **Kate** will come and visit in July.

_______________ 4. Juan wants to ride on **Jennifer's** horse.

_______________ 5. **Heidi and Jamie** rode the elephant.

_______________ 6. **Tom's** car was stolen from the parking garage.

_______________ 7. Julius gave **Tony** the book to read.

_______________ 8. Beth borrowed **Amy's** hockey stick.

_______________ 9. **The book** fell off the shelf.

_______________ 10. **The computer** constantly breaks down.

_______________ 11. **Louis and I** will go to the amusement park on Saturday.

_______________ 12. Anita found **shells** on the beach.

_______________ 13. Lucas took **Serina and me** to the concert.

Let's Describe It

An **adjective** is a word that describes a noun or a pronoun. An adjective tells what kind or how many.

Cindy has a **green** frog.

- Write one adjective to describe each noun.

1. flower ______________________
2. lions ______________________
3. pizza ______________________
4. breeze ______________________
5. boat ______________________
6. bike ______________________
7. bedroom ______________________
8. table ______________________
9. clown ______________________
10. ocean ______________________
11. forest ______________________
12. sun ______________________

- Underline the adjectives in each sentence.

13. It was a warm, humid summer day.
14. Jordan went swimming in the cool water.
15. The private lake was surrounded by tall trees.
16. He swam to a large raft in the middle of the lake.
17. Jordan dove off of the old, rickety diving board.
18. He felt a cool breeze as he surfaced.
19. Two friends joined him on the raft.
20. Yitzi was wearing his green and blue swimsuit.
21. Daniel had brought his new goggles.
22. They lounged in the hot sun telling funny jokes.

Commas Galore

A **comma** is used between the day and year in a date. Commas are used in a list of three or more words in a sentence.

Examples: I went fishing on June 5, 1994.

I live with a dog, a cat, and a bird.

- Underline the sentences that use commas correctly.

1. Bring me a pencil, a paper clip, an eraser, and a book.
2. Once I saw a bear, three cubs, a deer, and a raccoon.
3. Leon was born on May 12, 1984.
4. Lenia had a doctor's appointment on September 4 1996.
5. I ate a salad a roll, and a cookie for lunch.
6. Soccer baseball and football are fun to play.
7. Did you wash your face, brush your teeth, and comb your hair?
8. Natalie had her birthday party on August 17 1995.

- Add commas where they belong in each sentence.

9. Mother needs to buy lettuce carrots cucumbers and mushrooms.
10. The monkey snake and butterfly live in the jungle.
11. The book report is due on April 14 1997.
12. A triathlete must swim bike and run.
13. Maria had a dentist appointment on December 5 1996.
14. My grandfather was born on March 23 1940.
15. Halina likes to read jump rope swing and play chess.

Space Place

Space travelers from another galaxy can say many words, but do not speak in sentences yet. Write complete sentences that include the space travelers' words.

1. Earth has many big trees.

2.

3.

4.

5.

About You

A paragraph has a main idea. In many paragraphs, the main idea is stated in one sentence. The other sentences give details that support the main idea.

> **I love springtime**. The weather is warm, but not hot. The birds all seem to be making nests or feeding babies. Wildflowers bloom. I play outside more now that the snow is gone.

All of the sentences after **I love springtime** support this main idea.

Below are several main idea sentences about you. For each one, write three sentences supporting the main idea.

1. My friend and I have a great time. ____________________

____

____

____

2. There is one food I don't like. ____________________

____

____

____

3. Sometimes I daydream. ____________________

____

____

____

Mother and Father, May I?

Dear Mom and Dad,

A **paragraph** is a group of sentences that tells about a main idea. A persuasive paragraph uses details to help convince someone of something.

Think of something you would like to persuade your parents to do. Write a persuasive paragraph. Remember to indent the first word in the paragraph and use correct capitalization and punctuation.

Sea Creatures

In the reports below, look for the following problems:

- spelling
- punctuation
- capitalization
- misused words

Read the reports and circle the five mistakes in each one. Rewrite each report correctly on the lines.

The octopus is a see animal. It lives in the pacific Ocean and the Atlantic Oshun. The octopus has ate arms. it changes color when it gets excited.

an interesting feature on a starfish is its arms. The arms help the starfish sea. The starfish can regrow an arm if one is broken of. Under each arm their is a double row of small movable tubes?

How to Get There

A table of contents lists information about what is in a book.

Table of Contents

Answer each question by using the table of contents above. Fill in the correct answer.

	True	False	Can't tell
1. To find out places to see, I should turn to page 91.	○	○	○
2. If I like to take my time getting somewhere, I should begin reading on page 71.	○	○	○
3. Flying is my least favorite way to travel. I could skip the chapter beginning on page 1.	○	○	○
4. *On Land* ends on page 31.	○	○	○
5. If I do not like to fly, I should read the chapters that begin on pages 11 and 31.	○	○	○
6. If I like to get to places quickly, I should read the chapter beginning on page 71.	○	○	○
7. The Statue of Liberty is interesting to see.	○	○	○
8. *On the Water* ends on page 30.	○	○	○
9. *Sightseeing* ends on page 154.	○	○	○

In Its Place

A thesaurus lists words that have similar meanings.

Circle a word in each row that has a similar meaning to the **red** word. Use the thesaurus below.

sleep	slumber, doze, nap, snooze, drowse	**hide**	conceal, cover, mask, disguise, camouflage
slow	leisurely, unhurried, plodding, lazy	**make**	create, build, produce, form, manufacture
talk	converse, confer, chat, gossip, discuss	**pull**	haul, drag, draw, tow, lug

1. **make**	destroy	produce	demolish	wipe out
2. **sleep**	walk	snooze	awake	busy
3. **pull**	push	thrust	haul	shove
4. **hide**	exhibit	reveal	show	disguise
5. **slow**	fast	plodding	lively	swift
6. **talk**	listen	silence	chat	employ

Fill in each blank with a clearer, more interesting word. Use the thesaurus above.

7. We will ____________________ with the other team about rescheduling the game.
talk

8. Please ____________________ the bread dough into a circle.
make

9. Mom will ____________________ Dad's birthday gifts in the attic.
hide

The ABC's of Dictionaries

There are two guide words at the top of each dictionary page. They show you the first and last words listed on that page. The rest of the words on the page fall in alphabetical order between the guide words.

Pretend each list of words is from a page of a dictionary. Write the words in alphabetical order. Circle the words that would be guide words for that page.

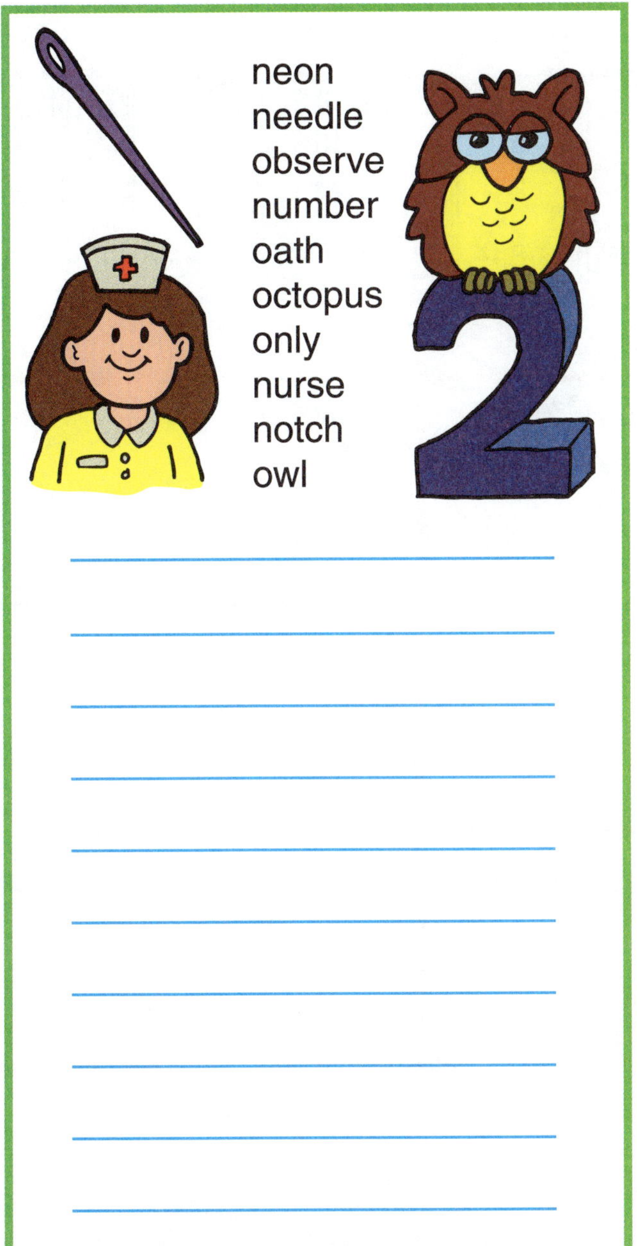

Letters and Numbers

An encyclopedia is a set of reference books. Each book has a number and a letter on its spine, or side. The letter on each book tells you that topics beginning with that letter are inside. Pictured here is a set of encyclopedias to use as a guide to answer the questions on this page.

Read each sentence. Underline the topic. Write the number of the volume in which you would find this topic.

1. What is a geyser? ______	2. How many legs does a spider have? ______	3. What is a nova? ______
4. Who invented the telephone? ______	5. What is an agouti? ______	6. What is the tallest tree? ______
7. Where did Velcro come from? ______	8. What are the primary colors? ______	9. What is the capital of Ecuador? ______
10. What is the population of China? ______	11. How is glass made? ______	12. What is a quetzal? ______

Understanding Maps

Symbols are drawings that stand for important things on a map. Here are some symbols you might find on a map.

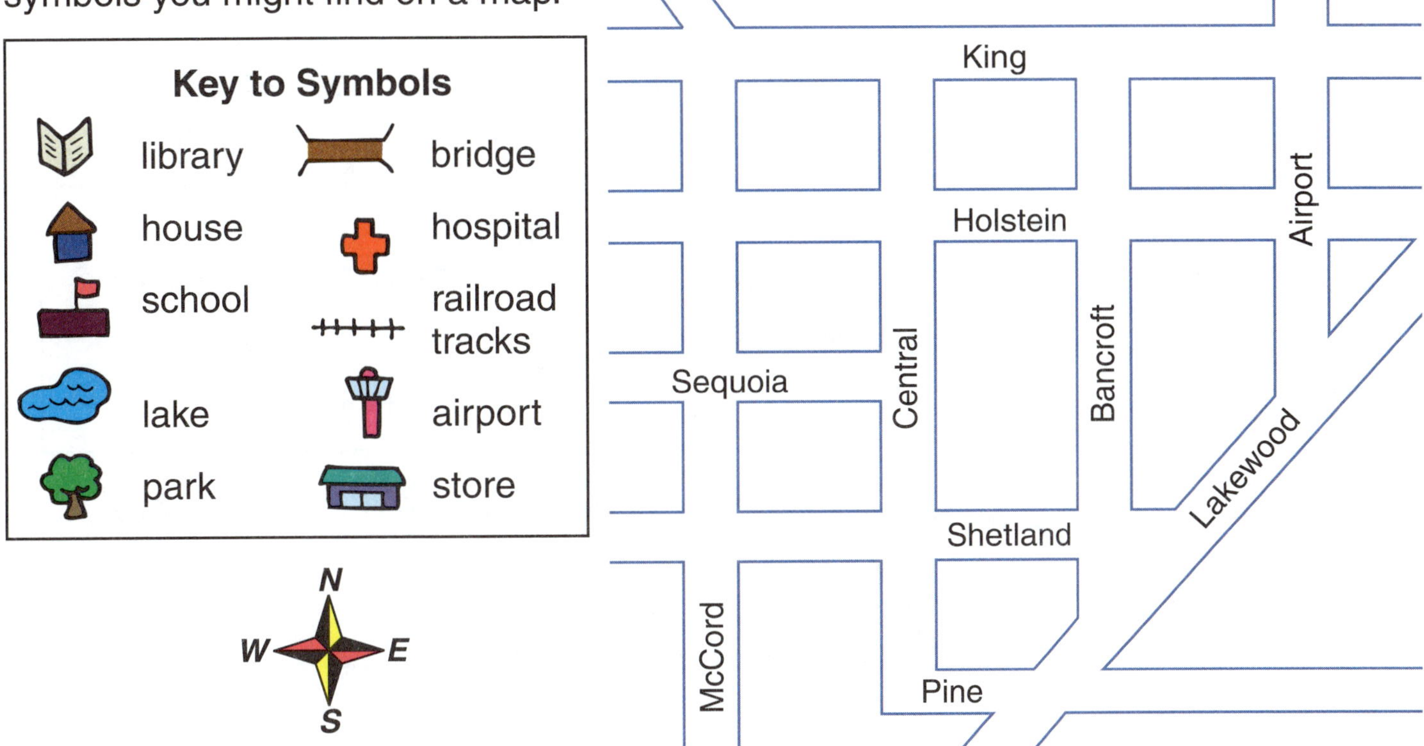

Follow the directions below to draw the correct symbols where they belong on this map.

1. Draw the school symbol on the east side of Bancroft between Holstein and King.
2. Draw the hospital symbol on the south side of King between McCord and Central.
3. Draw the railroad tracks symbol down the middle of Lakewood.
4. Draw the library symbol on the northwest corner of Central and Shetland.
5. Draw the airport symbol on the east corner of Airport and Lakewood.
6. Draw the store symbol on the southwest corner of McCord and Sequoia.
7. Draw the park symbol on the south side of Holstein between Central and Bancroft.
8. Draw the bridge symbol on Pine where it crosses over the railroad tracks.
9. Draw the lake symbol east of Lakewood.

A Trip to Bear Country

Here is a road map and a legend. The symbols on a map and what they mean are shown inside of a **legend**. Looking at the legend will help you read the symbols on a map.

Use the map and legend to answer the questions.

Legend

Bear Lake
Grizzly Mountains
river
Bear Cave
Cub School
road
Bear Cub Pool
camping
blueberries

Grizzly Town
N
W
E
S
Kodiak
Bear Junction
Bear Branch Village
Brown Bear Village

1. Where could the bears go camping? ____________________
2. What direction would the bears travel to go from the school to the river?

   ____

3. In what town do the cubs go to school? ____________________
4. Where could the bears pick blueberries? ____________________
5. In what town is the pool? ____________________
6. If the bears were at the lake, which direction would they travel to get to Bear Branch Village? ____________________
7. What direction are the mountains from the cave? ____________________
8. What direction is Kodiak from Bear Junction? ____________________

Answers

Page One

The following sentences should be underlined:

1. An owl is a kind of bird.
2. Some animals are reptiles.
3. People can buy bread at a store.
4. Chicken is a type of meat.
5. A pen pal is a person who writes letters.
6. Some books tell about real people.
7. A spider is an animal with eight legs.

The remaining sentences should be circled.

Page Two

1. fact
2. fact
3. opinion
4. opinion
5. fact
6. fact
7. opinion
8. opinion
9. opinion
10. opinion
11. fact
12. fact

Page Three

1. escaped.
2. went in to see the pup.
3. chased the cat.

Page Four

1. a statue
2. a musical performance
3. rider
4. a large rock
5. a meeting with someone to get information

Page Five

Word Box—uneven, disorder, disobey, unplug

1. disorder
2. disobey
3. uneven
4. unplug
5. decamp
6. deplane
7. rebuild

Page Six

Word Box—marvelous, breathless, peaceful, bendable

1. bendable
2. marvelous
3. peaceful
4. breathless
5. courageous
6. dangerous; full of danger
7. timeless; without time
8. treatable; capable of being treated
9. wonderful; full of wonder

Page Seven

1. 3, 3
2. 2, 1
3. 2, 2
4. 3, 2
5. 3, 3
6. 2, 2
7. 1
8. 2
9. 2
10. 3
11. 3
12. 3
13. 2
14. 2

Page Eight

1. lad der
2. com pound
3. or bit
4. ham mer
5. pub lish
6. en ter
7. ar row
8. cen ter
9. gal lop
10. mus tard
11. 2
12. 2
13. 3
14. 4
15. 3
16. 3
17. 3
18. 3

Page Nine

Circled sentences:

1. Hiking in springtime can be interesting.
2. It's nice to have a pet.
3. Deserts are full of life.
4. Texas is an interesting place.

Remaining sentences should be underlined.

Page Ten

The following circles should be filled in:

1. all three circles
2. middle and bottom
3. top and middle
4. middle and bottom
5. all three circles

Page Eleven

1. leave
2. ate
3. happy
4. hid
5. angry
6. kind
7. walked
8. journey
9. helped
10. argued

Page Twelve

person—Travis, brother, Maria, firefighter
place—China, school, store, house
thing—hamster, eraser, bike, football

Circled words:

2. picture
5. clock
8. book
9. Balls
10. car
11. Mice
12. net

Underlined words:

1. Linda
3. Grandma
4. Patterson School
6. LaNell
7. Max

Page Thirteen

Words underlined once:

1. country, buildings
2. queen, dogs
4. family, vacation
5. picnic
6. pizza, ice cream
7. heart
8. islands

Words underlined twice:

1. Italy
3. Olympics, Norway, France
4. Grand Canyon
5. Saturday, Wildwood Park
6. Emily, Little Flower School
7. Doctor Smith
8. Greece
9. thing
10. place
11. person
12. thing
13. place
14. thing

Page Fourteen

1. We
2. The wildflowers
3. All the trees in my neighborhood
4. My favorite tree
5. I
6. One of my friends
7. Our neighborhood club
8. We
9. Mom and Dad
10. They
11. Mom and I
12. The bulbs
13. I
14. My friends and I
15. Jill
16. I

Answers continued

Page Fifteen

1–6: Answers will vary.
7. Alex
8. He
9. Jake and I
10. Alex's sister
11. She
12. Sue's talent
13. Math
14. My favorite fish
15. Tom and Kim
16. The two men
17. My neighbors
18. The library
19. The milk
20. The computer
21. Penguins
22. Steve and Jeremy

Page Sixteen

1. packed a picnic lunch.
2. rode his bike to his friend's house.
3. walked to the park.
4. played baseball.
5. ate peanut butter sandwiches and cookies.
6. climbed on the monkey bars.
7. live in Calgary, Canada.
8. build nests in springtime.
9. performs tricks with a rabbit.
10. got a new bike for my birthday.
11. is gray today.
12. sells ice cream.

Page Seventeen

1. drove
2. flies
3. eats
4. grew
5. splashed
6. cried
7. spin
8. galloped
9. cheers

Page Eighteen

1. he
2. it
3. she
4. her
5. they
6. his
7. him
8. her
9. it
10. it
11. we
12. them
13. us

Page Nineteen

1–12: Answers will vary.
13. warm, humid, summer
14. cool
15. private, tall
16. large
17. old, rickety
18. cool
19. Two
20. green, blue
21. new
22. hot, funny

Page Twenty

Sentences 1, 2, 3, and 7 use commas correctly.

9. Mother needs to buy lettuce, carrots, cucumbers, and mushrooms.
10. The monkey, snake, and butterfly live in the jungle.
11. The book report is due on April 14, 1997.
12. A triathlete must swim, bike, and run.
13. Maria had a dentist appointment on December 5, 1996.
14. My grandfather was born on March 23, 1940.
15. Halina likes to read, jump rope, swing, and play chess.

Page Twenty-one

Sentences will vary.

Page Twenty-four

In the first paragraph, the following words should be circled —see, pacific, Oshun, ate, it. They should be spelled as follows—sea, Pacific, Ocean, eight, It.

In the second paragraph, the following items should be circled —an, sea, of, their, ? They should be replaced as follows—An, see, off, there, .

Page Twenty-five

1. true
2. true
3. true
4. false
5. true
6. false
7. can't tell
8. true
9. can't tell

Page Twenty-six

1. produce
2. snooze
3. haul
4. disguise
5. plodding
6. chat
7. confer
8. form
9. conceal

Page Twenty-seven

List 1	*List 2*
needles	seal
neon	skunk
notch	soap
number	stingray
nurse	strawberry
oath	taxi
observe	television
octopus	thread
only	tiger
owl	torch

First and last words in each list should be circled.

Page Twenty-eight

1. geyser; 8
2. spider; 18
3. nova; 14
4. telephone; 19
5. agouti; 1
6. tree; 19
7. Velcro; 20
8. colors; 4
9. Ecuador; 6
10. China; 3
11. glass; 8
12. quetzal; 16

Page Twenty-nine

Symbols should be drawn on map as directed.

Page Thirty

1. Bear Branch Village
2. North
3. Brown Bear Village
4. Grizzly Town
5. Bear Junction
6. South
7. East
8. West